SOUL SCARS
Rising Phoenix

SOUL SCARS
Rising Phoenix

a poetic journey through time

STEPHANIE LODGE

PUBLISHING HOUSE
Sherman Oaks, CA

First Published by Lodgeks Publishing House, 2013
4230 Stansbury Avenue, Sherman Oaks, CA 91423
info@lodgeks.com
http://www.lodgeks.com

Copyright © 2013 Stephanie Lodge
All rights reserved.
ISBN: 0988984598
ISBN-13: 978-0-9889845-9-2

Library of Congress Control Number: 2013902735

All rights reserved. No part of this book may be reproduced in any form or by any means without permission in writing from the author, except for the inclusion of brief quotations in a review.

Text, layout and cover design by Stephanie Lodge
Edited by Angeleah Anton

Printed and Manufactured in the USA and UK by CreateSpace

DEDICATION

This book is dedicated to the light that
streams through me from the infinite,
for without it I'd have no words to
express my soul's experience
upon this page.

CONTENTS

	Acknowledgments	i
	Introduction	1
1	The Pounding Beat	4
2	Beneath the Covers	5
3	Eavesdropping	6
4	Roman Waves	7
5	Peddling	8
6	Nowhere	9
7	Model	10
8	Graduation	11
9	Shower Dance	13
10	Traveler	15
11	The Toy of Tomorrow	16
12	He	18
13	Garden of Eden	19
14	Indifference	20
15	Shirley	22
16	Late Night	24
17	Craving Permanence	25

18	Puzzling	27
19	Blind Magic	28
20	Just a Thought	30
21	Child Vixen	32
22	The Day of Yes	33
23	Faith	34
24	Fumbling	35
25	Game Boy	37
26	Is it?	39
27	Peacock Men	41
28	What He Means to Me	43
29	War of Two Like Minds	44
30	Pros	46
31	Dare	48
32	Journeys	50
33	Flowers	51
34	Labels	52
35	Cradle	53
36	The Ringmaster	54
37	Muse	55
38	Desert Dweller	56
39	Rush	58

40	The Pain of Posing	60
41	Diamonds	62
42	Pearls	63
43	Listen to the Silence	64
44	Details	65
45	Spotlight	67
46	Ink	68
47	Countdown 2000	69
48	Deserted	73
49	Stress	74
50	Encore	75
51	Mommy	77
52	Daddy	79
53	Like Family	81
54	Contemplation	82
55	Hidden Room	83
56	Thresholds & Beer Goggles	85
57	Wishful Drinking	87
58	Creep	88
59	The Inevitable	89
60	On Love	90
61	Invisible Love	92

62	Ageless Woman	93
63	What I Found for Christmas	95
64	My Artist	97
65	A.K.A. Never	98
66	Rejection	99
67	Latin Dance	101
68	Awakening	103
69	Scarred	104
70	Timing is Everything	105
71	Be Gentle	107
72	Oblivious	110
73	9-11 for Peace	111
74	Phoenixism	113
75	Sheltered Garden	116
76	Breathing	118
77	Sweet Scar	119
78	Benedict	120
79	Missing the X	122
80	A Single Girl's Mantra	123
81	Original Sin	125
82	Sea Urchins	126
83	Near You Again	128

84	The Phoenix and The Wolf	130
85	The Rhythm of You	133
86	Touch of True Desire	135
87	Says it All	137
88	Car Wash Day	140
89	Mad Man	141
90	Blessed	143
91	My Candy Man	149
92	Mental Magic	150
	About the Author	153

ACKNOWLEDGMENTS

I'd like to thank the following for being an integral
part of my soul journey and the birth of this book.

Firstly, my husband KJ Lodge, for the new last name that's
much easier to pronounce and for demonstrating what love
is in every form by always encouraging my creative force
to shine no matter the hardships. He is my sweetest blessing.

My mother, Suzan Bagdadi, for showing me that life is always
perfect no matter what and never to acknowledge otherwise.

My father, Ariel Bagdadi, for teaching me that I can be by myself
because I'm never truly alone, no matter how far the miles stretch.

Jim Higginson, for his codes of light that flow through my veins
and teach me science is always part of the spiritual equation.

My soul family and friends for putting up with the countless
transformations over the years and accepting me as I am in love.

Loveliest of all, my angels and spirit guides – specifically
Marisa Covella – for reminding me that I am both a
student and a master in every moment.

But mostly, I'd like to thank the words for
always showing up on time and with purpose.

INTRODUCTION

I have to say that this book would never have been born if it were my decision alone. Mostly because what is printed upon these pages are words that no longer apply to much of my thinking or my current reality called life as I know it anymore. However, what I realize in reading through some of these poems is that I've chronicled a journey of my mind in such an intimate and sometimes embarrassing way, that it would be challenging to find an excuse to not publish them. For I realize now that there is purpose in everything we do, even if it shows up decades later.

These poems span almost two decades of my life, focused mostly on the time when love and relationships were paramount in importance to shaping who I thought I was and what I had to say about it. It's interesting to me to see the progression of my ability as a writer, going from someone who was uniquely innocent for her age to someone who quickly thought she mastered adulthood, specifically relationship. I find it amusing now that mixed in, especially in the beginning years, was an obsession with mortality and the stories of those transitions that occurred around me and how I dealt with them through my poems.

Then you have the additional element of what I term 'light streaming.' Which adds a whole new dimension to this book, for it is inspired by the spiritual forces around me who helped me make this decision in publishing everything, as is, no excuses or omissions.

One of these 'forces' is a girl by the name of Marisa Covella, who I was in high school with and who transitioned via car accident only days before our graduation. We had a soul connection that no one truly understood because it happened relatively quickly in our Senior year, bridging two groups or cliques that rarely spoke to one another. What I know now, that I didn't know then, was that we were connected energetically through the violet stream of light frequency that is so powerful and transformative. You have no choice but to connect to those within this same vibration. She was a huge fan of the color purple, even more so than I, who was still fond of blue then, but now I prefer purple as well. I believe it has something to do with our frequencies rising into consciousness, and hers was simply ahead of the rest. She came in very enlightened on a soul level to teach those she touched a valuable lesson – gratitude for life itself. Now in spirit, she is with me as a spiritual mentor and guide, helping me write this very forward and other books to come. She was one of my best friends during those early years, an artist like myself, and it was definitely a soul scarring experience to lose her and have to read the poem *Graduation* in her place at the ceremony a few days later. I remember racing through it, holding back the tears. I hated to speak in public then, extremely self-conscious and shy. She's helped me get beyond that since, and is still one of my best friends today. This is the power of the infinite, if you choose to tap into it and stay open.

To clarify further, light streaming means I channel directly from Divine Source or God or the Light Stream – choose your label – through my human filter and every poem in this book is a representative of that 'automatic' way of writing where words simply stream onto the page in an almost unconscious flow in a matter of a few minutes. Not one poem in this book took longer than forty-five minutes to an hour to write and most took less than fifteen minutes. Some clearly are better than others because of this fact. Ha! So, find what works, leave what doesn't. You'll see I rarely use punctuation, which is intentional, for it is up to the reader to decide a word's emphasis and create new meaning from there.

One poem in particular comes to mind as one of my favorites, it's called *Shirley*. I wrote it in a classroom in college about twenty minutes before my creative writing class. It came in out of nowhere off a memory of some *Aerosmith* video I saw. Not sure why, but its message still sticks with me because I wrote it word for word just in time for class and didn't think it was horrible. I remember a fellow student asking, "Where do you get this stuff?" As if he could mail order it. I answered, "I have no idea, it just comes into my mind and I write it down." Needless to say, he was irritated beyond belief. It was then that I accepted I might have a talent or a gift and that I should use it. It's taken me almost twenty years to step into being a published author, but I've been a writer in some capacity all my life.

You'll see within these pages that not all poems are created equal. But, regardless of how 'good' they may be, I left them relatively unscathed by my current critical, editing eyes in order to celebrate the evolution of the words and thoughts of my mind into a divinity of spirit over time. There is a lot of erotic flavor to this book because of the time it spans, and I am a Scorpio as well, which just adds a few extra 'shades' beyond '50' to the equation. It also explains the title a bit, since the Phoenix is one of the symbols for Scorpio. I am in a constant state of evolution, or 'Rising' as my spiritual guides put it, just as we all are.

Yet, the period of my life that was the most profound to me, in terms of carving my personality and leaving me a bit soul scarred, is definitely the two decades that span high school until I met my husband KJ in my early thirties. I am grateful they happened earlier in life, so that I could heal the scars that decorate my soul and I'm even more grateful that these poems still exist to catalog that journey.

So, this book is not simply a cute book of poetry I feel like publishing for kicks and giggles. This is a glimpse into a very personal part of myself, left unedited, so that others can be inspired to reveal more of their sacredness without fear. I believe when we fear, we lose connection with love, and when we lose that connection with love, we forget who we are as part of the Divine Universe that is in constant communication with us in every moment. It is simply up to us to open that window within our hearts and minds to let the light in. This is the light I let in, without fully realizing it then, between the years 1989 and 2009. I hope you enjoy the journey as much as I did and that it provides a glimpse of what is possible to create when we get out of the way and simply allow God/Universe to work through us as us in human form.

Gratefully,

Stephanie Lodge

THE POUNDING BEAT
February 2, 1989

Climbing upon the bare back,
Hairs prickling my calves.
Heavy breathing forces me into
A rhythm, which has no melody.

Protected beneath my sweater
I feel the wind only on my face
Mane flying, whipping my cold skin,
I feel a chill slowly creep up my spine.

Nostrils flaring, sweat dripping.
His hooves dig into the ground.
Clumps of mud and grass
Fly through the foggy air.

Crushing leaves as we ride,
Jumping green mossy logs.
I dodge the low branches,
While he reaches for high ones.

Wanting more than a flight through
The meadow, which surrounds me,
I stop breathless and abrupt – Only
To find my spirit continuing to ride
Through the misty morning air.

BENEATH THE COVERS
February 17, 1989

Beneath the covers – breathless
Blood rushing,
Listening to the hum of the house.

Beneath the covers – restless
Eyes burning
Waiting for sounds of keys in the door.

Beneath the covers – lying
Stomach growling
Thinking of chocolate cake in the fridge.

Beneath the covers – hiding
Teeth grinding
Holding my breath and trying not to giggle.

Beneath the covers – silence
Body tossing
Awakening myself into my dreams.

EAVESDROPPING
February 25, 1989

Ear grows numb against the door
The drinking glass never seems to work
I try to find out what one shouldn't
Mumbled words and sounds
Practically asleep standing up
The door opens with a loud thump
Crashes against my face on purpose
Clear words blend with scolding shouts
I cry out in disappointment
Mostly in myself
Found out what I really
Didn't want to know
The glass my only buffer to the truth.

ROMAN WAVES
March 12, 1989

Crowds of Romans watch
As gladiators battle it out
Tall pillars create geometric shadows
Against the gravel and blood of the Coliseum
Stark white robes and leather sandals
Chariots circle the circumference of the arena
Men bark orders with intent to kill
A ship sails by along the distant Mediterranean.

A daydreamer awakes.

Fans of a sport watch
As men pound their hands against volleyballs
Large metal trashcans rise from the sand
Florescent bathing suits whistle at tight sweaty abs
Offer terrycloth towels and cold electrolytes
Cyclists catch a glimpse of the scene
Gliding along on a winding isle of cement
A yacht cruises by against the waves of the Pacific.

PEDDLING
April 2, 1989

The feverish
Peddling
Faster and faster
Dad's steady grip
On the back of the bike.
The squeaky
Humiliating
Training wheels
The unattractive helmet
Two sizes too big.

More distance behind me
Confidence surrounds me
Proud of myself
The breeze on my face
Cools my sweat
My grip on the handlebars
Grows tighter
Crashing against the cement
My body tenses
Tangled in my bike
I struggle to get up
Only to find a few scratches and
Dad waiting with a giant hug
With eyes full of worry and guilt.

NOWHERE
May 7, 1989

Young men out on a ride
A short one through a canyon

Over a cliff in two point two seconds
Wasting seventeen years

An intelligent boy with a future
Changed instantly into a past

His future – a hospital bed
Filled with nightmares and hopeless dreams

Brain damaged forever
No longer really alive

The young man gave up his life
To take a short but fast ride

A teenager with a seemingly
Indestructible body and mind

Wasting a brilliant future and
Possibly that of his friends

These tire tracks lead to nowhere
They only blow away with the wind.

MODEL
May 9, 1989

Just another pretty face
One with a gorgeous smile
Gone from the human race
She was driven that final mile
Acting of every sort
Mostly modeling
Hopping on a plane somewhere
To be
Photographed or
Attend some fling
Her last goodbye was smashing
I mean that literally
Her body went down crashing
Jumping
Fifteen stories.

GRADUATION
June 25, 1989

The stroking of the ivories in a repetitious melody
Marching down the isle in our caps and gowns
Hearts full of an unbearable excitement
One full of accomplishment and heartache

We already miss high school in some ways
The teachers, the friends, the experience itself
What we could get away with as teenagers
We now know must be given up as adults.

We had our decisions to make
And we've made them
We have our dreams to fulfill
And hopefully will fulfill them.

We look around at each of our classmates
In an almost disbelief
The ones we disliked, the ones we never knew
But, mostly the ones we loved.

The tears begin as we watch each other
Rise and receive the diplomas
Our future handed to us neatly rolled
Tied with ribbon, then sealed with a firm handshake.

The accomplishment and memories are ours to cherish
Our youth as we knew it draws quickly to a close
Moving our tassels from left to right – we stand.
We are the class of Nineteen eighty-nine.

SHOWER DANCE
March 8, 1990

Parched skin of baby powder
Soaks up the wet sprinkles
Caught within rainbow walls
She dances among friendly tears.
Naked child
Tiny fingers and toes
The faucet god provides the magic
In her emerald eyes wide
Blond hair blows innocently
Dragged gently through the morning
Breeze of water.
Blades of grass softly cut her feet,
Unseen villains squirm quietly beneath
Then everything ceases.
She stops spinning along with the world
Shower dancing is over
Weeping into the soft, warm terry cloth
Serenity and safety in her mother's arms.

Wall Street woman awakens
Far from her home and her rituals
With only her memories bringing her back.
Tasting bittersweet on her tongue
Somehow today her car doors seem thinner
The smog blacker or air thicker.
Somehow today the safety is all gone

Only paranoia in a turbo world
Alone or in numbers irrelevant.
She sits and waits by a phone
While the world speeds up
Leaving her behind in stillness
She's stopped spinning once again.
The fatal ringing her final confirmation
Destroying her hope, her protection, her home
All her serenity and safety
Warm and soft washed away
The shower dance is over
Soaked up under the blades of life.

TRAVELER
May 18, 1990

Invisible support to the winding isle
Arms reaching for some unknown destination
Lights magnified tenfold by fog's breath
Hurtling through the mysterious monster
Pink Floyd echoes off the moment.

Darkness embellished by growing mountains
The wheels turning in slow motion
Eat the dashed aisles of smooth pavement
Tattoos of yellow and white on black skin
A concrete Mohawk separates direction.

Occasional escape offered into the marked unknown
Safety in numbers turns deadly to the chosen few
The ghosts of passengers linger in the cool air
Hiding behind curtains of oozing cloud
Waiting to make their entrance.

Rush to squeeze through warps of wind
Between the space of teeth to your own destination
Adrenaline fuels you past everyone else too quickly
Wait for time to catch up with you
Or you may arrive too early.

STEPHANIE LODGE

THE TOY OF TOMORROW
November 21, 1991

The last one
A dead shriveled seed
Our only hope of a new
Survival
Swept away by
Religion, government, US
Five, Four, Three
The first seed of steel
Filled with new destructive juices
Giving birth to our death
Hundreds, Thousands, Millions
Vanish among chemical clouds
Some even before they appeared
Blown away by deserted winds
Silent and dry
Ashes of life dust swirl uninterrupted
Tornadoes of screams unstoppable
Two
Bodies thrown across each other
For years like lovers,
Only death survived their ecstasy
No seeds
No babies crying hungrily
No more threats of
Disease
War
Hunger

All is done
No canopy beds for little girls
Toy trains for little boys
Only a single switch
To the biggest toy of death
A bomb
The sun kisses the ocean's profile
One.

STEPHANIE LODGE

HE
February 14, 1992

He smells of sincerity
On a cool summer day
Wise thoughts of passion
Tender nibbles of intellect
Maybe just an hour
Or a day
Or maybe a lifetime.
My love tastes of warm musk
Dawning in the evening hours
He caresses my emotion
Drowning my sorrow
With the sweetest laughter.
The pedestal to the sky of my mind
More than a princess in his arms
I dream of him often.
My love sounds perfect
Yet isn't
For perfection is adrift among
Superficial mentality
And he dwells within substance.
My love is beautiful to me
Graceful movement
Hidden by very real stability.
My love is mine alone and
Always will be.

GARDEN OF EDEN
June 12, 1992

I'll be your truest fantasy
Still, remain myself as well
We'll find our core's tranquility
Hidden among night's stars
Encased in waves of sky
The pulse of our fingertips embraced
Will guide us to a shore of bliss
Without trees, nor flowers, nor earth at all
Faith is our support, love our beauty.
Maybe not forever, maybe just a blink
Yet a single blink of your eye equals
A million in mine, an eternity.
Crying from the top of our lungs in silence
Or whispering an earful of screams
Here there's no noise, only music
Here there's no hatred, only freedom
It grows on the walls with no gate
We're here – now – this is it
This feeling of confusion
With no feeling at all
This is the Garden of Eden
A place to live with ourselves
A world to live with each other.

STEPHANIE LODGE

INDIFFERENCE
January 12, 1993

His lips dance upon my back
I weep
Always hiding his face from me
And his feelings
In the darkness of life – our love.
I just hear his breath – the mask.
Brushing aside my hair with gentle fingers
His wind whispers in my ear
Melodies of inaudible words
That are erotically meaningless
I miss him from yesterday
What was isn't what is – now.
My needs – a vacant lot
Waiting for refreshment
Yet I stay because it's easier
My emotions – they grow harder.
I feel colder
Like stormy fall breezes that etch their way
Through my bones and into my
Blood – cold purple.
Sad phone calls – empty receivers
Quiet dinners by frozen candlelight
No words left to say
So we say nothing, do nothing
Just sweep our thoughts under the bed.

SOUL SCARS: Rising Phoenix

His name is Indifference
We met a year ago
And he prefers to dance alone.
He's happier that way – safer somehow
Sometimes I stare into those windows,
Whose panes seem swollen with sorrow
The glass dull from it's constant wiping.
Hoping, searching for a thought
That isn't there, and never will be.
It's buried deep – lost within his fears
From the world and me.
Love does escape through
Climbs a way out
But pain is trapped, forced to linger
Like a caged panther gone mad.
Softly the sorrow grows stronger
And I – I just sit and wait for tomorrow
The phone to call out my name
Hearing his voice
Searching for yesterday like mine.
Yet still frightened of losing
The fragment of today that dwells
So I wait – listening to his breath
Then silence – then the magic "I love you."
That once erased every scar on my back
But now just rakes the wounds
Like thin cat claws on sunburned skin.

SHIRLEY
April 4, 1993

When they said beauty is only skin deep,
Shirley was never in mind.
Her hair – waves of yellow straw yarn
Framing blank blue orbs of
Limp gelatin and fragile glass
A large snout protruding over scaly skin
Bleeding red matte lipstick – dry, caked
Peeling like old tattered cellophane off
Frog lips – pursed into a dime-size circle of skin
The blotchy sandpaper complexion
Painted by childlike hands
No art involved, no style, just Shirley.
Nothing natural about her building
No inhabitants either
Just arms, legs, sagging breasts left sitting on a potbelly.
Even her ears – scarred with too many holes
"Poor girl, wonder if she'll ever marry?"
That's all they said, enthralled and appalled
Like scared dust running from a vacuum
But meant to enter
Then suddenly her cracked lips move
She speaks.
An odor of jasmine from her words, warm and sultry
Like molasses.
The music of jazz or blues in her talk – spellbinding.
Shirley knows how to work what she's got

A gift, though poorly wrapped, once opened it shines.
Still, those eyelashes like daggers
Eyebrows of painted arches
But she talks.
Angelic, beautiful words.
Springtime air and warm sheets
Poetry flowing from her tongue
Silk.
The clothes – dull, five and dime
But those words erotic
That voice melodic
What deception to those few lonely minds
Calling her Roxanne or Lori
Listening to dripping honey over a phone
Nine-seven-six who knows her?
They only know what they hear
And assume what they want
Shirley knows how to work what she's got
And well.
The gift of illusion
A magician of pleasure
No sight, no touch or taste
Only sound.
Her voice – the loneliest of them all
Home – some small plywood desk and vinyl chair
Fruit loops and the times
A cord with a one-way receiver.

LATE NIGHT
April 17, 1994

Pillows left abandoned on the hardwood floor
Snuggling partners sprawled across the bed
Swimming under fluffy goose down and flannel
Saliva dribbling from between his pink lips
Charcoal mascara smeared under her eyes
Looking like a football player.
More comfortable, less glamorous, relaxed
The clock reads two a.m.
The glowing television moves dead light
Across their bodies and the dark room
An overhead mirror reflects moving images
Then a slight rustle from an arm or a leg.
The late night dance begins, sudden toss of a head
Throwing tangled hair across distorted faces
Window blinds sneaked slightly opened – unnoticed
Surely dawn will wake them come wistful morning
Dreams are meanwhile bridled by obnoxious noise
Sounds of info-crap like *Hair Club for Men*.
Finally a hairy arm struggles and stretches
Frantically searching, then grabbing the remote
Too many buttons that barely work
The moving images now somewhere in black tubes
Quickly sucked back into the TV where they came from
Leaving the snugglers left to pursue their slumber.

CRAVING PERMANENCE
May, 1995

Craving the noise from above
He drove east
The pain in his arm still numb
Drug cruising through his veins
No longer driving in neutral
His destination is close
But to him still so far
The cold steel encasing his body
Seeps through the windows
Melting into a small clump of
Death next to him
On the passenger seat
The machinery simple
His mind of butter
Still aware of the final ritual
Wheels grab a lonesome spot of
Highway
Desert gravel
He stares long into the
Silhouettes of cacti and mountains
Alone with his drug and the
Terminator
Tired of himself
Tired of running
Too wasted to know better
Years spent sleeping

Escaping his hell of nowhere
The juice is fading
He sucks in another needle full
Elastic pinches his fair skin and thin hairs
He settles back
The glowing sky slowly disappearing
The loaded machine waits
Then the noise he craved comes
Launching him into his
Permanent rest.

PUZZLING
June 7, 1996

Features swirl in front of my mind
But I can't remember the face
Like a puzzle with no matching pieces.
Blueberry spheres
Surrounded by soft lashes of lace
A silk smile to surrender to
His hair simple but different.
I'm so overblown by the effect
I can't focus on the actual image
His large build is strong
His style embraces his mood
Perfect.
He notices my friendly stare
And shares it with me
Like a nice bottle of wine
Oblivious to our friend
Introducing us.
Our hands never touched hello
But somewhere within us
We held desperately to each other
Embracing with a comfortable hi.
I felt him listening
To my every word
So I tried to be cute and funny.
Until next time we meet
I'll keep trying to finish the puzzle.

STEPHANIE LODGE

BLIND MAGIC
October 14, 1997

Blessed with blindness
His love is a magic that's truer than most
Hello, my magic man
I am your dream queen
So nice to meet you again

The fantasy begins softly
Breathing flows between moist ears
I am stirred by a sincerity of a stranger
Our insanity and fear keep us tuned into
A channel of make believe and loving words

We merged at the necessary moment
Needing reassurance and acceptance
Chosen to fill our appropriate voids
Healing the scars that left us empty
Oblivious to the inner temporary

Our sight is slowly returning
To a reality we fear but accepted
He worries that I may be right
That all is lost when given sight
To the true identity of our farce

But I have faith that my heart
Will retain the magic of this man

His graceful, beautiful, and tender core
Keeping me blinded by the truest love
A dream queen could ever hope for.

STEPHANIE LODGE

JUST A THOUGHT
November 5, 1997

You know that thought, don't you?
Last one you ponder before
Dozing off to unbridled dreams
And the first one in the morning
That sneaks into your brain
Unannounced
Just a thought
Just an image
Those shoulders, lips and eyes
Forcing you awake at seven a.m.
Pounce
Like a hungry cat meowing you to feed him
Not letting you escape back to sleep
Swimming in circles in your brain
Yes
That thought.
Remember now?
The one that says loud and clear
Oh god, you're in so much trouble
But you love it, don't you?
Don't we all?
So you just lie there
Soaking it in – for the fiftieth time
Enjoying the possibilities
Savoring the Kodak moment
Knowing eventually

When slumber comes to you
The wake up call may be less
Shall we say...stimulating.

CHILD VIXEN
November 22, 1997

Child-woman with bee-stung mouth
A throwback to some 20's film
Appearances deceive.
A sheltered flower that bloomed
Into legs of malleable steel
Breasts of warm vanilla pudding
Raw filth tied with pink ribbon.
She emanates a sex appeal that is subtle
Bubbling beneath a pristine surface
Daring you to stare too long
At lashes that seduce
Careful
Could be hooked by soulful eyes
With handcuffs glistening behind them.
Velvet sheets flow from between her lips
Visions of ruining her make-up
With passionate juices
Painting with hungry tongues
An erotic art of forceful strokes
A delightful bond of creative brushes
Dip slowly beneath the wet surface
Painting lips red with thoughts of love
Could be worth it.
Molding her into your woman-child
Mouth stung by your affection.

THE DAY OF YES
November 24, 1997

Yes
It'll come
Not today
Maybe not even tomorrow
But eventually
Yes

I know you're waiting
Patiently
Politely
Okay, not too politely
But that's understandable
Someone like you
Alone for some time
Wanting not to be
I understand
I do

So, yes is all I can say
A promise of sorts
Unless of course you
Screw things up
And I'm forced to say
No.

FAITH
December 11, 1997

Knowing
Deeper than blood running red
Through veins of twisted hope
Blindly feeling a truth that
Exists purely in minds of history.

Trusting words of prophets
People that heard a voice
Wrote it down with instruction
Answering our needs
So we continued asking

Confusion sets into damp minds
Sweat on furrowed brows
Which think too hard instead of
Following intuition
Better than acceptance of all.

Fear outweighs logic
Power of faith isn't always healing
It creates an excuse to stop wondering
Instead of us realizing life isn't perfect
Or, for us to know completely.

FUMBLING
December 17, 1997

Eager to please
With puppy kisses
Tickling wars begin
Flirting with enrapture
He's not eager to start
What she won't finish
So he thinks

Unfortunately mistaken
Self-control his specialty
Oblivious to her intent
To finish what she started
Hands can be wonderful tools
If used correctly
A concern of his

But she won't let him in
On the secret – not yet
She enjoys the fumbling
The stumbling into walls
A foreign hand exploring
Investigating on it's own
Her James Bond wants a clue

But she prefers him
Both shaken and stirred

STEPHANIE LODGE

Spying in unknown territories
Dangerously close
To discovering something
Of himself inside her
Pretty sex machine.

GAME BOY
December 17, 1997

Twisting words around delicate fingers
Which probe beneath the fragile surface
The message isn't transmitting clearly
Blind woman feels his face
Tunes in with a squeeze of an earlobe
Just a girlie toy for this game boy?
Maybe.
Too many buttons to push
Not sure how to play him
Hard or soft
Hot or cold
Spicy or sweet?
Maybe all six
Not used to playing these games
Never have in some ways
He knows
Takes advantage
Guess he likes the upper hand
Too careful with his words
Where she shoots straight with her hips
Random romantic bullshit
Oozes from hungry lips
Thinks she likes to hear it like his other
Little girls waiting in the wings
He's dead wrong
About many things

Doesn't have the time to look behind
The curtain of a giggling façade
Who's really naïve here?
Won't find out until it's too late
Sport boy isn't so quick after all
Doesn't remember her rules
Funny how things can turn around
When you're running after something
Stumbling to regain your footing
Is he playing to win or what?
Guess she'll never know
The game is over
Before it truly began.

IS IT?
December 18, 1997

Is it always going to be about sex with you?
Is it just what I can do to you?
Is it going to change anytime soon?
Or should I just get used to it?
Is it ever going to mean more to you?
Is it just the convenience of me that's important?
Is the fact that you like me enough for you?
Or do you think you'll eventually want more?
Is the fact that I could want nothing annoying you?
Or the fact that I could just do you and walk away?
Because I could if I needed to
If I felt there was nothing to make me stay
I have learned to become indifferent to the male mind
And that's what bothers you more than you'd like
That you may want more of me than just a casual fling
You may like me more than my pure sexuality
But you don't want to have to decide – not yet
You like my neck dangling from your string
Waiting for the phone to ring
Unaware of the scissors hiding behind my back
Sorry, but I need some answers now Jack
I would rather cut that cord with you
Then walk the rope between for now and forever
And if I decide to label you
Cut any emotions from this point on
You'll be just a body to me and nothing more

I won't be able to love you
I'll be forced to close that door
So I guess it's up to you to decide
To either gamble with me or run and hide
Share the possibilities please
What you know and what you see
But most importantly
Is it even meaningful to you how I feel?
My questions, my wants and my needs
Because if not my dear boy
There are plenty of other plastic toys
With hungry mouths to feed.

PEACOCK MEN
December 21, 1997

Come on
Touch it
Why,
It's the eighth wonder
Of the world
Didn't you know?
Faster than a speeding bullet
More powerful than...

Yeah, yeah
Enough already
You're shedding feathers
All over the bed
You don't need to do your
Little dance for me

I said it's not little.

Length
Girth
Whatever
There's another muscle
More important than
That piece of knockwurst...

Oh, come on

STEPHANIE LODGE

Wish I could
Really
You peacock men are all the same
Emphasis on the "pea"
If you know what I mean
You should know that's
Not what us birds rely on anymore

It's the beak and how it pecks
That really matters

Really?
Hmmm.

Any offers manly man?
Or don't you think you can handle it?

Maybe.
But only if you let the
Locomotive do some chugging too.

I'll see what I can do.

WHAT HE MEANS TO ME
December 28, 1997

Soft places of tenderness left to explore
That's where he waits for me.
A hesitant walk through an open door
That's who he seems to be.
Craving the fullness of his magic mind
That's how he feels to me.
Willing to taste it one bite at a time
That's what he means to me.

STEPHANIE LODGE

WAR OF TWO LIKE MINDS
January 11, 1998

Heat concentrated inside a marble of flesh
Ready to explode at the thought of his smell
Thoughts of him touching her with his tongue
Bring warmth and moisture to her lips
He doesn't kiss her nearly enough
She just longs to feel good
He won't allow it
Gives her a crumb or two to nibble on
But not the entire loaf to devour as she pleases
She brings him to his moaning place
With puffs of hot air along his neck
Tease
Groan
Grind
Pinch
He won't touch her the right way
On purpose she's sure
She touches him too much
So right, it's wrong
They won't give what the other wants
She won't stop
He won't start
He doesn't like to show his passion
Fears it might be stolen from him
She waits for complete annihilation
Her arsenal of garters and panties wait

A war of libidos rages through pulsing veins
His canon is armed and dangerously close
Her walls are high but crumbling slowly
The rain and fog clouds their vision
Boom, boom, boom, boom!
The war rages on into midnight's open arms.

PROS
January 13, 1998

Kissing
Tracing his lips with my tongue
Open mouth
But not for long
He fills me with his softness
Nibbling my bottom lip
Tickling my teeth
Robbing me of fluid
So thirsty is he
I let him drink slowly
Feeling the breath on my chin
My neck
My ear
Then exploding back to our mouths
Pushing to some other side
A dimension of things to come
Teasing each other relentlessly
I know this is all I can afford to give him
Of myself and my spirit – for now
Unsure if it's enough to keep him
Kissing and tracing
Nibbling and tickling
Robbing me of my essence
Drinking and exploding
Pushing to be with me
I'm left with the label of teasing

He's left hoping for more of me.
We're professionals
In the art of
Waiting.

DARE
February 2, 1998

Do I?
Can't afford to
Not with a heart so raw
Swollen from the
Wringing of tissue
Opens damp salt wounds
Wish I could though
Does he?
Not before me
I think
Dodging rosy arrows
Afraid to get stung
Just to have the bee
Die after all
Avoidance of pain is a
Tedious process
Gutless beauties of passion
Hold tight to flannel pillows
Wishing for nerves they
Do not possess yet
Shouldn't
Until the time is right
To express with words naturally
What bodies already heard
Through touches so soft
Strokes so tender

A moment so still and tense
Chilling the warmest of spines
One special place that never changes
With time or age.

JOURNEYS
March 2, 1998

Wandered long into the horizon
Knowing not the heading
Found a spot of sunshine in my way
I pulled my lids down tight
Then hoped that the brave night
Would swallow up the day
Cradled in the cool moist air
Fear still settled in my brain
Stumbled over thick illusions
Of cemented hills crumbling
Left to crack in their decay
Feeling melancholy and abandoned
I crept into a cave of solitary
Then worried I would never be found
So I crawled back to the sunshine
Pulling it aside like a curtain of gold velvet
Found a piece of evening developing in raindrops
Photos of lost stars, clouds and sky
Space was finally within my reach
Just over the moon, beyond the beach
Now all I needed was wings to fly
But I settled on quietly lying down instead
Dreaming of more journeys inside my head.

FLOWERS
March 16, 1998

A simple gesture of something to come
Though no one should really expect them
A dozen or more is the rule of thumb
Yet, sometimes just one is the method.

Bouquets of fields and laughter
Can brighten the darkest of rooms
A simple tulip or budding rose
Can banish the heaviest gloom.

For romance is hidden among the petals
Tenderness flows through long stems
A healing scent that could warm metal
Wishes that glow to the heavens.

But the best of them all is one from the heart
Whether it's rose, tulip or jasmine
A bouquet, just one or a plant in a pot
They're thoughtful
They're beautiful
They're magic.

LABELS
April 16, 1998

Miller Genuine Draft on brown glass
Take off the label
Could you tell the difference
Between Rocky Mountains
Or Ice Brewed?
Maybe you could
But I doubt it.

Gucci, Donna Karan, Calvin Klein
Cut out the labels
Could you tell the difference
Between basic black suits
With plastic buttons?
Maybe you could
Maybe you couldn't.

Black, Hispanic, Asian or White
If you shut off the lights
Could you tell the difference
Between the feel of their skin
Or the smell of their breath?
Maybe you could
Maybe you shouldn't.

CRADLE
May 7, 1998

Light my way to rooms of velvet curtains
Walls of paisley passion
Cradle me in quilts of woven warmth
Sunny days lead me to your front door
I find the key under the rock behind the stairs
You let me in
Trusting touches of faded poetry
Written on your skin
Exposing you to my fresh canvas
I paint you with pale colors
But save vibrant red for your pouting friends
Separated by a probing tongue
You let me in
But only briefly.

STEPHANIE LODGE

THE RINGMASTER
May 9, 1998

The lamest show on earth
The clowns with many faces
Invite you to their tent of fools
Him leading them in paces
They don't perceive him as the one
The ringmaster of the family
For then they wouldn't have their fun
In watching him act loudly.

Like a tiger caged with bars of steel
He treads a ground that's broken
His heart is left as his last meal
The final scrap – a loveless token
He swallows the pain once again
Hope still lingers – the show will go on
But still the answer lies in when
The fools will finally admit they're wrong.

MUSE
May 10, 1998

Mind wanders to a field of torn grass
Cutting gentle fingers with shallow lines
Quietly undressing the earth below her feet
The blades tickle between painted toes
Hair flows down
Caught between pouting lips
She brushes it aside easily and smiles
You call out to your inspiration of talent
Your voice lost within the gusts of wind
That dance in a ballroom of green waves
She turns her back and runs from you
Afraid of losing her, you awaken
Finding her gentle fingers
Intertwined with yours
The shallow lines growing deeper
Allowing you to sleep once again.

STEPHANIE LODGE

DESERT DWELLER
June 18, 1998

There's this man I know
From the desert

He's in a desert still

His home of serenity and sunsets
Is where his soul prefers to dwell

Afraid of torrential downpours
Flooding his fears of emotion

He finds the dryness suits his needs
Better than the calmest ocean

The air that he breathes
Just mingles with that of God

Clean with honesty and candor
He exhales light and love

Even when his truth is painful
Like chafing hills of sand

His hugs are urgent and filled with need
Proof at heart he's a loving man

No matter how much venom lingers
Within collapsing veins

He chooses to always make amends
With every scorpion and snake

This man will never be a cowboy
He doesn't need strength to survive

He simply thrives in his blooming desert
Happiest with his new son and wife

I know him better than most
For I've devoted much emotion and time

To find a place within his heart
That doesn't hurt my mind

He will always be a valuable man to me
Even though his desert chills my spine

Because as a father who did his best to love me
He is mine.

STEPHANIE LODGE

RUSH
June 26, 1998

What are you afraid of missing?
When you fly by at 80mph
Everyday
Not an emergency
Just everyday
The rushing
The stress of traffic in your bones
It's getting to you
It's making you mad
Those red lights staring at you
Behind other angry drivers
Like yourself
Your life has got control
You lost it back there at Wilshire
Where you hit a woman in the face
With a sting of a middle finger
How lucky are you going to be?
Everyday
Not just today
But everyday
The *almosts* will catch up with you
Then faster than that light
You chase
Your ride will be over
With death's embrace
Metal upon metal

And not just yours
But some random human
Smoking Marlboros
Enjoying waves of Cashmere
Their foot on the brake
As you plow into their everyday
And take it away with your own
No more potholes to distract you
No constant groove of paved cement
No radio stations
No destinations
No everyday torment
Just a memory
Of a rush you no longer possess.
In the end
Your fear of being late for life
Will be all that you have left to miss.

STEPHANIE LODGE

THE PAIN OF POSING
July 1, 1998

We rummage through identities
Looking for the perfect fit
Afraid of being who we really are
Wanting to be loved
By majorities of people
Who rummage through identities
Of their own.
Standing with over-priced wine
In plastic cups
The illusion begins its display
The black turtlenecks discuss
Some stock they should possess
On hot summer nights in LA
Sucking on their cigars with
Penis envy or oral fixation
Oozing behind yellow teeth
"Oh, I just love the taste"
Is all they can say
They watch the tight dresses
Fly by with their silicone searchlights
Hungry for cash to impress
With nowhere to go but the bathroom
Hoping someone will want to
Talk to their breasts
They'll drive home in taxis
Their tiny wind up toys from Japan

An embarrassment to valet.
As the lights come up at 2a.m.
Tight dresses scramble like
Cockroaches for the door
Afraid to be seen in direct light
Their faces might melt away
While the true beauties go home alone
Disgusted with the night's posing
The black turtlenecks stand drooling
Smell and sweat under their Hugo Boss
Cologne hovers around and through them
They dream of their "nice girl"
A wife and a mother
But take home the shortest of skirts
Who come at high prices
And come often
So the cycle continues…
A night in the life of L.A.
How it hurts.

DIAMONDS
July 6, 1998

The strength of a diamond
Depends on the incision of its shell
Similar to the strength of the mind
One must look between the cuts
Through the windows to the soul
To see what beauty they can find
Often brilliance is reflected
Enlightenment revealed
Two prisms subtly intertwined.

PEARLS
July 6, 1998

Women wear many kinds of pearls
Some dangle from graceful necks
Other lace feminine curls
Maybe an earlobe, or maybe two
Sometimes upon a finger
Nails painted blue
All of them feminine, strong and true.
Strands of them drip from a delicate wrist
Or are squeezed between two
Voluptuous breasts
Still, the mother of all pearls
The most feminine of its kind
Lies hidden between
Two quivering thighs.

LISTEN TO THE SILENCE
August 19, 1998

Silence
Like being underwater
So deep you can only
Hear your blood flow
Unable to breathe on your own
Where blue becomes black
And white is never known
Eyes can't focus where
Light won't reflect
Hands can't touch when
All they feel is the same
This is where the angels swim
This is where they sing
Their glorious hymn
Haunting us with memories
Of moments stretched over
A drum of time
And when they are through
Our beating done
Once again we appreciate
What the silence can do
And listening has begun.

DETAILS
August 23, 1998

An auburn hair trapped by
Jaws of flaking
Fingernails

Splitting under cotton candy pink
Flakes of polish
She pulls it like a thread

From the eye of a needle
It sends a chill to her inner thighs
Before falling to the floor

Grinding
The sand paperboard
Blends the layers

Levels the off-white enamel
White dust landing in her lap
She brushes it off to the floor

Molecules of her life
Scattered
Pieces left for a vacuum

To absorb into its dust world
Eyelashes, skin, mites and sand

Races mingling over cocktails
Of ashes, lint and hair
Resurrected into the air
By blowing machine

Returning to her lungs
Uninvited microcosm of her
Existence.

SPOTLIGHT
August 23, 1998

Tears through my flesh
A heat of splendor
Reaches the bone
Then bounces back
To you

Radiates colors of gold
My prism soul of fame
Turning my emotions
From lightest silver
To darkest blue

Flashes photo rays
A spying eye of public
Peeling off my skin
Exposing each layer
To the many curious

Dies in small notes
The music fading softly
Into background vocals
Of rumors and melody
No longer furious.

INK
September 19, 1998

Fear tears at me
Stripping away my flesh in layers
I'm naked to myself
Forced to see what I reject
Confidence on the verge of vanity
I back away from my defenses
No one sees me for my talents
They focus on an exterior
I meet them halfway
The shy girl I once was
Must now put her dolls away
The thoughts of being average
Are not an option and long gone
Like the dust blown off an old letter
Torn and frayed around its edges
Stained with coffee spots or tears
From a frightened writer
Exposed with black ink.

COUNTDOWN 2000
September 20, 1998

A child's eye view up black leather skirts
Silk blouses tucked over sexy lingerie
Gold chains dripping off necks
Suicide was in fashion then.
Scars hidden by diamond tennis bracelets
Helmet perfect hair carved in Vidal Sassoon
Mousse teased to balding at the roots.
Hair spray rock of the eighties
Bowie's little china girl uninvited to
Idol's white wedding.
Teens hungry like a wolf for their MTV
Video waves bouncing money into pockets
Of tight pants and T-shirts
Miami Vice never looked so good.
Remember when Michael Jackson
Was a black boy trying to be a man?
Instead of a man trying to be a white boy

Blowjobs of powdered sugar
Sweet caution of sex still hidden under
Mirrors and black satin sheets.
Fast cars parked in herds
OUTSIDE Club 54.
The place NOT to be seen.
INSIDE the place not to be sober.
Swatches and the Gap on every

Pimple faced punk groupie dude.
Valley girls and their rubber bracelets
Invented hanging at the mall.
Too young to appreciate
The speed of life passing them by.
Their parents driven numb by the ride.
Enjoying less taxes on their homes
More reasons to celebrate
Up 'til three a.m. and late to work again
Until...

The Nineties hit like a neon Concorde
Arriving before departing late.
Leaving us holding tickets to a destination
Of super model fashion and granola hair.
Of Nirvana spread with Pearl Jam
Smashing Pumpkins screaming off key
Anger bought by the hundreds.
Of an artist formerly known as Prince
Remember Purple Rain?

Of crank and crack who overpower
Their grandfather cocaine.
While humble heroine continues to
Fry juvenile brains
Who now live on the streets
Homeless from eighties' reign.
Hookers and pimps still at war
Some things never change.

Of cautionary sex
Injections of many kinds
Juxtapose a disease like Hollywood
No thought to race, age, sex, talent or minds.
Of sports utility vehicles
Churning more gas into fumes.
Of coffee shops and pubs
Private lists to shoebox clubs.
Of freeloading celebrities
Returning worn out Gucci shoes.

A child views the debt it must pay
Of a world party it was never invited to.
The path is set.
Television our leader.
While the President sits back with his cigar
Thoroughly getting screwed,
Children rush through college for a job
In order to feel the pressure lift
Off young shoulders.
They die for fear of what else
Will be stolen from them.
Protecting themselves down to their shoes
With automatic guns and branded tattoos
All because of abandonment issues.
What therapy can never do is remove
The anger of the burden we all possess.
Divorced parents
Who married too young

Partied too hard
And left love buried under
Mortgages and credit cards.
They watch as their children
Do it all wrong
Not married at all
Having babies who look forward
To a future faster than any we've seen yet

Millennium could equal Armageddon
According to Nostradamus.
If we never learn to slow down
Embrace the stillness of our beings.
Instead we worry about
Meteors and aliens invading the earth
Earthquakes and floods ruining our homes
Tornadoes and hurricanes blowing our spirits away.
Our only challenge left is God
Our ability to learn to pray.
Not some HAL computer
Or other sci-fi fantasy film.
When 2000 comes
We start at zero
Square One
Hopefully we can repair
The damage we've done.

DESERTED
October 22, 1998

The desert of his face said everything to me
The sand slowly dripping from piercing eyes
It blew across the dunes of his cheeks in circles
Into his mouth oasis - sucked bone dry
The grit caught hold between chalk teeth
Forcing a smile older than a thousand years
I stared in pain at his deserted face
Unable to quench its thirst with my own tears.

Powerless to drown his inflamed passion
His memories lost to an abandoned vastness
One that evaporates the stormiest rain clouds
And dries up oceans in fear of growth
Then suddenly the sands just blew away
In search of a new shore to caress
I worried the desert heat would overtake him
Until he found mountains to undress.

STRESS
October 23, 1998

Slithers up the legs to the spine
Coils up in the small of the back
But just for a minute before it unwinds
To travel further to the base of the neck

Squeezes tightly uninterrupted
Forcing you to take a deeper breath
Then splits into two smaller versions
One for each temple above the ear
Pulsates like a beating heart
Continues this for what seems a year

Until you find that magic potion
Hiding in the back of a drawer
Hit two back with a jerking motion
Then slowly ooze onto the floor.

ENCORE
October 27, 1998

Pen and paper act as my props
My mind the stage
Using words for my cast
I begin my production

The curtain slowly rises
Only to find
An idea not yet constructed
Into a set

I direct my characters
Blocking
Their entrances
And exits

Finding myself
Blocked
Into
One idea

Trashing
Wads of paper
I waste my humble
Magnificent crew

Rehearsing

STEPHANIE LODGE

Through draft after draft
I finally give up
Finding the curtain slowly closing.

MOMMY
November 3, 1998

I'm sorry this thank you is so late
It wasn't meant to be
I've always been bad at this
Haven't I?
All your sacrifices for me
Unappreciated.
Seventeen hour work days
Breaking your back
With weekends of
Taking me to horseback riding
Singing lessons and modeling
Wanting me to learn who you
Were and wanted to be.
Through observation and admiration.
I did rub your back
I remember that.
Sore from standing endlessly on stages
Lugging groceries up stairways
Even when he left
You did these things with purpose
Always my companion
Loving me regardless of my faults
The hurtful words that flew out of my mouth
Like stinging bees escaping a broken hive
You knew the honey hiding beneath
Even if you didn't always get a taste
I thank you for that

For always sticking with me
I'll carry that upon my wings
The day I choose to fly away.

DADDY
November 3, 1998

I feel lonely sometimes
Knowing how far away you are
Remembering the days
When you'd come rushing in.
Keys hitting the counter
By the back door.
The breeze of you flew by
Up the hall to the back den
Checking urgent messages
Left by those hamster voices
Screeching numbers and demands.
You were always in a silent rage
The rush of life choking your smile
Into fits of "where's my..."
I was your Sherlock Holmes
Finding socks and lost keys
Hidden by the back door
Under some paper
Just where you left them
Unseen like me.
As you rush out again
The door slamming
The breeze gone
Echoes of those blustery days
Stay with me into
Calmer nights

STEPHANIE LODGE

Finding myself
Losing my keys
By back doors or under papers.
Waiting for someone to
Find them for me.

LIKE FAMILY
November 6, 1998

He looked at me like a sister,
But didn't always
The romance flew to Paris or
Somewhere with warm beaches
I was untouchable to him
His patient fantasy overworked
I trembled in grief at being thrown away
The shivers slow and deep
Like the pressure of a spinal tap
The needle pulling out your core
Through bone marrow and blood
Until I realized he was right
I never felt that magnetism
Just a fondness sprinkled with
Flirtatious sexuality
So what did I expect but
A family friendship
Flown in from somewhere dull
Like Minnesota suburbs in winter
Or somewhere with frozen ponds
I had looked at him like a brother
And always had
Leaving only one to be broken hearted
And one just guilty of incestuous thoughts.

CONTEMPLATION
November 6, 1998

Counting bathroom floor tiles
Every crevice memorized
How much time wasted?
Flushed down a toilet
With imaginary conversations.

HIDDEN ROOM
November 10, 1998

I can always count
On your snide remarks
Hidden behind those
Thick tortoise frames.
The ones you're trading in
Any day now
Oh yeah, any day now.
If you ever decide on
Their replacement that is.
You don't think I can
Hear your little comments
Swimming in your brain
Hidden poorly behind
Quiet soulful eyes.
But, I'm not deaf
Maybe you didn't know that
The way you seem to stare
As if studying some
Abstract painting you must dissect.
Something new on my face
At least to you I guess.
Still, I'm shaken by that laugh
The one you feign to control
On my behalf.
Simply because it brings in doubt
Invites it in

STEPHANIE LODGE

As if sitting and talking
Was some new sin.
Then there's that certain look
Yes, there's a certain look.
That always comforts and reminds
Why I come to this room
Every day now
Every day now for several months.
Because among the world of gloom
We simply share our minds
And for me at least
That's reason enough.
Until that day I'll look up
To notice you've had quite enough.
No more studying or staring
With that certain look with soulful eyes
Hidden poorly behind thick tortoise frames.
I'll be hurt, maybe surprised
But, then I'll simply walk away
Comforted by the truth that remains.
Certain friendships bloom
In the strangest of rooms
Growing into poems for friends
That mark beginnings and maybe ends.
But until that day
Who knows? Could be soon.
I choose to stay
In this hidden room.

THRESHOLDS AND BEER GOGGLES
November 18, 1998

Remember that time you met someone
Simply stunning in thought
Ravishing in intellect
A sparkling sense of humor
You could talk to this person for hours
Or longer even
Except for that one item
Physical attraction
It lost its invite to the party
And forgot to bring beer
You strained to find features to
Focus your attention on
A wave of hair woven
In between fried ends
A hazel prism hidden under
Mud brown eyes
Maybe a straight smile
Covered in yellow slime
You couldn't do it
Couldn't ignore the obvious
To find the obscure
No matter how hard you tried
It was like that damn solicitor
Calling during dinner
You knew you weren't going to buy
Still, you were polite

STEPHANIE LODGE

Took the phone number
Or gave them yours
Wasted a few more cordial words
Then searched the room
For something more magnetic
Knowing the ravishing, stunning and
Sparkling individual you left behind
Would take several more Coors to digest.

WISHFUL DRINKING
November 22, 1998

I wish you were water
So I could sip you
Drop by trickle
Trickle by drop.

Until my mouth was full
Of your inner workings
Who you are and
Who you aren't.

I wouldn't thirst for
Secrets locked away
I'd consume them all
By the end of the day.

And when I was drunk
From drinking you in
The quench of your soul
An unfulfilled sin.

Would filter through me
Leaving a hole
Flushed away
Via toilet bowl.

CREEP
November 23, 1998

Drooling like some hungry dog
Dripping in his beer
He sees me sitting like a log
Praying he won't come near
But, of course he must approach
Crawling slowly on his belly
Like some sluggish cockroach
His breath and clothes all smelly
I try to turn a little bit
But, he is most persistent
Thinks he'll impress me with his wit
Then I become resistant
This ticks him off to no end
Like he's some Valentino
He mouths some words that do offend
So, I drench him in my vino.

THE INEVITABLE
November 23, 1998

Howl at the desperate night
Stare at the shallow moon
Twinkle with fire delight
Stars still spell doom.

Age with the rustling trees
Swallow the nighttime sky
Lift mountains with burly ease
Pigs still won't fly.

Cry for your earthly mother
Sleep in her velvet womb
Search to find some other
Creation is still your tomb.

ON LOVE
November 23, 1998

Nothing to say but this.
If it doesn't happen to you
You aren't ready.
When you are
It will come knocking
Like the Grim Reaper
For your soul.
But, this time
It doesn't take you away
To some dark place
It leads you to sunshine
Kissing your face.
With petals of lips
Twinkles of fireflies
Trapped in your heart
Their glow easy to recognize.
They shouldn't complete you
Just let them be
Keep them warm and safe
It's what works for me.
And as time passes
When you feel you can share them
Release a few to the air
To let the wind carry them.
To open hearts empty
Needing a glow

For sharing of love
Is one's ultimate goal.

INVISIBLE LOVE
November 24, 1998

Ever lay in bed alone
Wishing you weren't
Dreaming of him or her
Snuggled in your chest
Having sweet conversations
With an empty pillow?

Ever hold tight to that person
The one you haven't met yet
Longing for their kisses
Coaxing love from their heart
Quiet tantrums beating softly
Until your sanity falls apart?

Ever want to find them so much
You see them on a street corner
Imagine that they see you too
But instead of asking who they are
You slowly walk away so far
That only invisible love shines through?

Me too.

AGELESS WOMAN
November 30, 1998

She was spent
Like a dollar bill
Transferred from grimy palms
To dirty pockets
From New York to Sydney
The consummate world traveler
Wrinkled and creased
Faded from washings
In pockets of jeans.
She was tired
Like the excuse
Given by a cheating husband
Believing his own lies
Having said them so often.
Looking in eyes of disbelief
Tears welling in corners
Where a light should be
Exhausted with himself.
She was lonely
Like a seashell
Sitting on a beach
Waiting to be picked up
Washed off
Emptied of ageless sand
Then displayed proudly
Among the other knickknacks

Still lonely on a shelf
But, safe from the elements.
She was gone
Like the wing tips of geese
Withdrawing from view
On a horizon of sunset
The black slowing dwindling
To a distant speck of pepper
As the yellow rays swallow it up
Until one must look away
Retinas burned by the brilliance
Reflected in ageless eyes
That has seen enough life
To last hundreds of years.

WHAT I FOUND FOR CHRISTMAS
November 30, 1998

I thought about it for a long time
The gift I wanted to give you
For Christmas and
For all the other days of the year
I kept thinking what could symbolize
My feelings for you?
Surely not some cashmere sweater
Or a watch with glow in the dark hands
No, it had to be something better
Something richer than money or chocolate
Deeper than the darkest reef in the Pacific
Stronger than some steel chain
Lifting the anchor of a battleship
The gift that would make you
Love me as much as I loved you
It of course couldn't be my love
Since you had that already
It couldn't be my heart either
You already held it in your hands
Then all at once it came to me
What would make you happy?
The hardest gift to give you
The easiest one to find
Your freedom pure and simple
To love me as you choose to
On Christmas and

STEPHANIE LODGE

Every other day you had in mind
Knowing that no matter what
Whatever size your love could be
I would be completely satisfied
Since your gift fits me perfectly.

MY ARTIST
December 3, 1998

There were tears hidden
Behind the smile
The tears that I could only see
Having seen them many
Times before
No one knew you like me
No one saw the misery
Swimming in your eyeballs
Blinking through them
At the ugly world
Until one day it took you
Suddenly - too soon
I'll meet you there someday
When my job here is through
And now when I look to the sky
See you painting me sunsets
Of purples and pinks
Wrapping up the sun for the night
Cozy like we were
Sitting in your living room
Munching on Red Vines
As I think of our memories
My smile is tremendous
Even if no one sees it
Hiding behind lonely tears.

A.K.A. NEVER
December 7, 1998

When the Middle East finds peace with religion
And the Christ returns to give us back our sins
When the chimes of Big Ben stop ringing
And the Pope has sex within the walls of the Vatican
When the dunes of the Sahara flatten to plateaus
And the cliffs of Dover crumble to the ocean floor
When the women stop wanting security in life
And the men stop wanting sex every six seconds
When the children stop pretending to be grown-ups
And the babies stop crying when they're hungry
When the rain stops pouring everywhere in the world
And the waves fail to reach the sandy beaches
When the moon stays full and behind the sun
And the sun spits water instead of fireballs
When the comets lose their tails of ice and dust
And the stars implode to nothing all at once
When the sky turns yellow from pole to pole
And the clouds disintegrate into empty atmosphere
When the trees curl up into their roots
And the continents stop drifting apart or together
When the core of the earth solidifies
And the volcanoes harden from the inside out
That's the day I'll stop loving you
And when your meaning to me I'll forget.

REJECTION
December 29, 1998

Two emotions lived together
Fear and Love
One day they made a baby
His name was Rejection
Now, Rejection preferred his mother
Love
She gave him courage
She gave him self-esteem
But, his father controlled him
Wanting him to grow up in his image
And unfortunately
Rejection was always a good student
Then IT happened
One day he wandered into the street
A bus approaching unseen
His mother, Love
His father, Fear
Stood together nearby
But only Love could move
She rescued him from the bus
Holding Rejection in her arms
Soothing him with warm words
Fear just watched unable to budge
So, that day Rejection grew up
He realized that to accept his father
He would never live up to his full potential

What his mother had always taught him.
So, he decided to change his name
and became Acceptance from that day on.

LATIN DANCE
December 29, 1998

I found you standing taller than me
A feat in itself
In the corner with a woman
Her back to me
Her wavy long hair glistening
In the candles' whispers
Across the room
I stood dumbfounded that she
Found you first
Her thick accent tempting
But not enough to distract you
From my stare

You saw me wander away
Then chose to follow
Gliding with your size fifteens
Until I approached with my silly
Question
The one I hate to answer myself
Height is such a boring subject
Isn't it?
But you were nice
With your easy way of talking
A Miami flare hiding underneath
And boy could you dance

We danced with the freaks

Falling into their oblivions
You liked to sing certain songs
In my ear
Holding my hands
Close to you
And then the music softened
Drawing us closer to ourselves
Then with a kiss
You were gone
Leaving me to wonder
When you'd call
If ever
But, you didn't
The dance was done.

AWAKENING
January 26, 1999

The lace of winter black branches
Against a hazy blue paper skin
Chills felt where leaves had been.

Mountains scratched the horizon
With a French white manicure
A bracelet of river tumbled cool and demure.

A single scar of sunset
Amid blisters of clouds
Ready to burst with a misty white shroud.

The mirrors of lake reflected back to me
What I had already known I guess
That there didn't exist a man who was blessed.

Not one heart strong enough to love me
With more than just infatuation
For me, what a mind-blowing realization.

STEPHANIE LODGE

SCARRED
January 29, 1999

The sound of the scissors
Scraping hair follicles
Before falling to the floor
With my memories of girlish
Ribbons and ponytails
Leaving a boyish figure
Staring back at me
From behind warm tears
In a cold mirror of self-pity.

TIMING IS EVERYTHING
February 14, 1999

The door closed slowly in my mind
I wasn't quite ready for the room to be gone.
No more kind infatuation
No more teasing with flirtation
The friendship seemed done.
I'd like to say I was sad, but, I couldn't even sense it
A gentle numbness came over me instead.
All this time I had wondered what you were thinking.
Maybe fearing rejection, or were you just
Annoyed with me inside your head?
I know I ignored those looks
Too often to count on both hands.
The ones that whispered foreplay
While I pretended they didn't.
All the times I saw frustration creep into your brow
The guilt of being unfair still runs on indefinite.
I know you've tested the waters many a time
With those quiet soulful eyes
Staring behind new round frames.
The ones that still calm my nerves and remind
Why I can't just walk away.
But, knowing your fear made it mine too
So, erasing it with hints of interest is all I could do.
Sometimes I just float like a sitting duck
Unsure of what to say to you
But, I just can't call your bluff

Now that you've left me here
Without my hidden room.
Things just don't seem the same
There's an uncomfortable gloom
Some say if you stare sixty seconds or more
You risk fighting or making love.
I think that margin drops to thirty, or maybe even ten
When you look at me that way.
The intensity heats me to the core
So much so, I'm forced to look away.
It's strange how fear and love
Go hand in hand when they are such opposites.
It reminds me of the possibility of us
Though now I'm just frightened
Of your final response
Or maybe it's my answer to it
That I fear most of all.

BE GENTLE
April 13, 1999

I think of you often with fondness that splinters
Into memories of stolen glances, like those old forties films
You asked me for the fiftieth time
Are you wearing splash? What's it called again?
Rainwater? Sunflowers? *Sunwater*, I reply.
To a man whose memory grows dim
Then the twinkle of your eye tells me
You knew the answer all along
I guess you still like to flirt? Is that it?
Not directly with me though
Just the thought of possession
For a moment, or an evening, maybe longer
But it's doubtful to you, isn't it?
I'm not exactly her, am I?
I don't have the blond curly hair
Just down to there...do I?
I'm probably a little taller than you imagined too
Still, the eyes might be nice; after all they're blue.
She probably has more curves to her body
A touch more color to her skin
Not the alabaster glow I've been living in.
All of these revelations, you think they slip my mind
But no, no... I've imagined just your kind.
So here's a hint
She's standing behind another door that's locked
But, meanwhile you found a key in me.

That you'd probably like to use
To unlock some pent up fantasy
Alleviate yourself from being bruised.
I let you because I'm free to without the strength to stop you
Still, maybe you should concentrate past proportioned lips
Legs a little too long for you, attached to stronger hips
The blue eye shadow you requested that smudges easily
And two dimples behind a frown that you strain to see.
Instead look at a woman inside hiding
Behind a thicker, harder door
Afraid to show a softer side that leads you to her core.
For fear you might like it better, or reject it for its sin
So either way you taste it, she will never win.
And she hates to be the loser
Only one thing hurts her more
The act of being chooser
Only to greet a slamming door.
She'll wear her life upon her sleeve
To build your confidence
But, you must move quickly
Your chance is only once.
However, you decide to stare her down
So that she can barely breathe?
She stutters to close her open soul
Before it gently flees.
And then it's back to square one
Don't you worry, she's not angry
After all is said and done
How could she be?

For who's to blame for having fun
'Til true love comes knocking quickly.
I know I'd rather eat the sun
Than walk the moon indefinitely.

STEPHANIE LODGE

OBLIVIOUS
May 8, 2001

He likes to torment me with
His devilish gaze and
Satanic smile.
Convinced it's erotic foreplay
I acquiesce.
His hands and mouth are my
New best friends
Seemingly knowing my erogenous
Zones for years.
He plays with me against warm sheets
Fuzzy sofas and marble showers
I'm consumed by thoughts that
Verge on illegal, but mixed with
Emotion that's tender and kind
And to think
He was right in front of me
All of this time.

9-11 FOR PEACE
September 11, 2001

Today we suffer for all of humanity
We suffer for our country and our planet
We suffer for innocents lost mercilessly
We suffer for children who are now orphans
We suffer for families too shocked to grieve
We suffer for our souls, their light dimmed.

Today we must celebrate an opportunity
The opportunity to glimpse our true potential
To see that what we're up against is not just external terror
But, the internal terror and fear that exists in our minds
We must replace it with light and start manifesting peace
We are all love and light and not separate
It is up to each of us to remind those who have forgotten
The shift begins today and this is our reminder
How vulnerable not only our country has become from within
But, how our planet and its soul need healing
Now is our time to heal it
It is time to live a higher truth
It is time to evolve together to something larger than ourselves.

This tragedy has affected all of civilization
But, from the ashes will rise the Phoenix once again.
To soar to greater heights of peace
Stronger than thousands of white doves
We must focus on our potential

STEPHANIE LODGE

As planetary healers and bringers of light
We are all the light and love we need,
Bring light to those lost in darknes.
Bring air to those who barely breathe
Bring comfort to those who have lost their sense of peace
Bring strength to those who need new courage and heroism.

Our lifeblood has been cut savagely and deeply
By small minds, dark hearts and lost souls.

But, it can heal and it will through unity
Unity of prayer, thought, word and deed.
We will see a brighter future for our planet
We will manifest a greater love that is immune to terror
We are human, but we are also of a light
That's greater than our minds can even imagine
Find it within your soul and in others
Share it with those who need healing and forgiveness
Make that choice today.

Lets remember this date as our
Country and our world calling for
A state of emergency
A planet in emergency
We must listen and answer that call
Will we listen? Will we answer? All of us?
We are the healers. We are the hope.
I know we will.

PHOENIXISM
January 22, 2002

It's torn
The image
No longer
Perfection
Never was
Didn't know it
Until now
And there's no
Scotch tape
For this.

It's hard to
Hear our music
Amid the noise
Of judgment and
Confusion
When we prefer
To always speak
Than to listen for
The melody
Of our song.

Fear lurks in
The shadows
He worries
So do I

Because life
Has no guarantees
And we'd rather
Destroy a love
Then let it destroy
Us.

But it won't
It can't
It doesn't know how
Love can only teach us
About ourselves
About each other
About how to love clearer
Brighter and less afraid.

I've already learned
The hard way I admit
To stop proving
Something
Anything
Nothing at all
To him or to me
To stop worrying
About tomorrows
That might never be.

And like the Phoenix
We both know too well
We'll rise from this ash
Learn from our mistakes
Erase dark thoughts
And find new pathways.

It takes work to mend wings
It takes work to fly higher
It takes work to learn
To see that no hearts
Are broken
No hurts are left unhealed
No bones are left
Bruised by painful words
Our love will
Burn brightly
With new wonder.

I have faith in that
It takes work to say
I was wrong
I'm not afraid to work
With you
Please forgive me
And let us rise again
To a new song of hope
A new melody of us.

SHELTERED GARDEN
February 6, 2002

Let me shelter you
Your spirit
Your mind
Let me take your fears
Your worry
Your doubt
I'll replace them with love
A healing
That's tender
And kind
Then the light from within you
Will find its way out.

Let me shelter you from
The storms of your life
Protect your hopes
Your visions
Your dreams
Then you'll find the
Worry vanishes
Doubt dissolves
And your growth as
Spirit
Manifests before me.

Let me shelter your heart
As you've sheltered mine
Let's share the growth of abundance
Through the universe divine
We'll watch a garden emerge without
The thorns or the weeds
Only blossoms of joy
Is all that we'll see.

Let us all share in the
Wondrous realization
That the world can experience
Lifelong transformation.

BREATHING
June 21, 2003

Take me with you
To the place
Where fear becomes love
Past failures erased

I know the way
But would rather follow
Trusting your footsteps
My mind becomes hollow

I want to fill it with poison
That numbs the pain
So that I can avoid
Going insane

Because try as I might
I can't replace
The thought of his lips
Kissing my face

So give me your hand
And tell me you care
Because hearing your voice
Is like breathing in air.

SWEET SCAR
January 11, 2004

Breath on my face
Sweet scar of mine
Where are you tonight?

So far away you fade
Into stars above Paris
While mine hover LA.

Mine dim against a grey sky
Covered by fog of regret
Do yours glow brightly?

So far away you burn
Even if you can't feel me
My heart beats soft and warm.

Whisper just one more word
A single syllable will help me
Speak our language tonight.

While far away you drift into
Words stumbled over coffee
Awkward moments left undone.

Maybe I stole you from the
Dream of a fallen angel
As his feathers dissolved into air.

STEPHANIE LODGE

BENEDICT
January 11, 2004

So easy it was
That night
Under the heat lamp
That we didn't need
To keep us warm
We had our joy instead
My giggles mixed with
Your goofy laugh
Perfectly in tune
Our lips played the music
As people left the room
One by one into just us
Two smiles
A rainbow complete
We danced to the music
That didn't have to play
Our bodies still in sync
My spirit recognized yours
Almost immediately
My mind waited to make sure
But, then she penetrated us
A witness to our perfection
Wanting us married
Right there
On a carpet dance floor
In a room full of strangers

We knelt down
Drunk on wine and lust
With vows we don't remember
Except for the "I do's"
Our souls intertwined
In a marriage divine
Lost in a moment of now
I was yours and you were mine
But, neither could say how
Then our wedding night
A torture of frozen feet
Human blankets tangled
I wanted you inside me
Feeling your warmth
Painful like a virgin
Until I realized you
Weren't there to hurt me
Relaxed I let you in
And watched your face
Open with pleasure
I was now inside you too
Your soul my treasure
And when we awoke
Our rainbow filled the room.

MISSING THE X
February 18, 2004

Your energy pulled away too soon
I was just beginning to get a buzz off of you
Damn the frog in my throat
The tears in my skull sucked back
My tune is just so out of whack
I got used to our harmony
The music of our conversation
The tremble of our bodies excited
But, suddenly your notes
They fall flat.
Over electric waves on my computer
Staring at the last email you sent
With just your name
No more love charm
Missing the X
That reminded me of your kisses
Safe and warm.

A SINGLE GIRL'S MANTRA
April 13, 2004

I miss you from yesterday
Pillows strewn across the floor
My mascara smeared
Looking like a football player.

Our battles were nice, weren't they?
Legs and arms wound tight
Flesh shaken and stirred like
A very dirty martini.

But, today my sheets are ice cold
My blanket chokes me
Reality TV numbs my brain
While I just think of your ass.

This isn't good
I need some medication quickly
Or a Venti soy latte maybe
Depending on my mood today.

I'm not sure where I'm going
When the freeway looks the same
Everyone with their cell phones
Causing Verizon wireless traffic.

Work will dull the crap out of me most likely
Same stale coffee breath emissions
From my assistant's verbal assaults
Warning of empty meetings with no purpose.

Then oh goodie, I'm off to the gym
Thirty minutes of sweaty torture
Followed by five minutes of complete terror
As I race through an empty parking garage.

My car chirps at me with security – how sweet
The *Soul Sessions* ooze from my car speakers
I have frantic imaginary conversations with my boss
Telling him to go screw himself for the eight hundredth time.

Uh huh, this is my normal now
My routine that I share with a half million
Other single women who have no patience
For single men who we just don't want to see naked.

So, yes, I miss you from yesterday
Because today is over once again
And you're still not here to keep me
From this hamster wheel of my life.

This freak show that has no intermission
Until I find a brave new heart to share
Quiet moments of passion and
Sweet nibbles of intellect.

But until then, I guess I'll just keep bitching to unwind.

ORIGINAL SIN
May 1, 2004

You are an original
An original sin
Where fantasy ends
And desire begins.

Connected by wires
Strung tightly by words
Your voice is magic
To the point of absurd

I want to taste you
Warm and inviting
Until I consume
All that's exciting

I've managed to wait
Patient and calm
But, don't make me hate you
By waiting too long.

STEPHANIE LODGE

SEA URCHINS
January 18, 2005

Balmy breezes through my window
I already hear the sand under my feet
Sloughing off cells that have never
Seen the world beyond
Imaginary countries of spices and jungles.
Two blocks away from
Waves of peaceful churning melody
Singing giggles and
Sandcastles aplenty.

Then I drift like wood
Eight thousand plus miles
To mud and debris littered with shoelaces of
Tattered children not lucky enough to be woken
By drenched nightmares of
Giant chasing walls.
They float in my dreams
Haunting drifting angels
Fingertips just out of my reach.

The survivors smile sweetly
Serenity comes through art and play
They draw blue pictures
Laugh and sing their loss away.
Proof that to be alive but alone is still miraculous
Even with ten years to rebuild

Their missing family and homes in front of them.
How do they do that so easily?
Day by day.

My struggles seem petty now.
My complaints smaller
My life bigger.
Lonely maybe, but not alone.
Orphans in life, but not spirit
Reminded me that inner strength and hope
Is more inspiration than a breeze or a wave
Could possess
This is what I might have missed.

STEPHANIE LODGE

NEAR YOU AGAIN
March 10, 2005

Your wrinkles are a bit deeper
But, the face the same
Rugged jaw and nose
Broken too many times
Your dimple manmade
By a fist and ring
Not a natural pretty boy, but
A sexy one just the same
And you're not mine
Not anymore
Though sometimes temptation
Creeps in uninvited
Inside my swollen brain
Puffy with memories of youth
Tongues tangled and lips secure
You were my *everything* once
Until finally security slipped away
Love in a death grip
As personality tore at us
Differences abused our
Sense of humor into injuries
We were unable to heal
Still I miss the gentle glances
I stole one tonight while you
Were pretending to look at a car
Passing on the street outside

Intensity under long eyelashes
Fixed me to you
But, couldn't fix or erase
The reality that you are still
As wrong as wrong can be for me
So, near you will have to be enough
I guess.

STEPHANIE LODGE

THE PHOENIX AND THE WOLF
March 21, 2005

He found her in a magic place
Her wings still shaking off
The last dust of smoke and ash
She had just risen again
As she did many times before
Her colors more vibrant
Her life more valuable
She was stronger now
But still aware of the beasts
That had caused her to burn
So as to recognize them again.

He snapped branches on purpose
Reluctant to approach with fear
One glance of her color was enough
As long as it was unfiltered and pure.
She stayed still and watched him
His warmth radiating from within
She knew there was no harm intended
No reason to fly away and escape
This animal was a curious puppy
Not the savage beasts wanting to devour
Her beauty to leave a shell of mistakes.

His tail wagged with enthusiasm
As her colors got more vivid to him

She was afraid the fire surrounding her
Might scare him away forever
But he knew how to build bridges
Ones tall enough to scale the walls
That both imprisoned and protected a heart
That was still sensitive from its recent rebirth
Its beating still rapid and nervous
With anticipation and hope for love
Could he be the one in possession of such a gift?

Then he jumped over the flames beside her
The heat licking his belly softly as he
Landed in her world of make believe
Where pain is disguised with perfection
Because she never knows who will pass
With ridicule and judgment on the agenda
Here the ground became more dangerous
No leaves or twigs for him to snap
No sounds to comfort or control
So he rested a bit and regrouped
Fur against feather kept them warm.

He woke to the sound of thunder
An angry train rolling above him
It was time to seek some shelter
From a possible onslaught of rain
So he looked at this bird beside him
Realizing a decision had to be made
To crawl to his bridge and take her

Or let her fly away to a safer place
For he thought with the rain came freedom
From the challenges of this fire between them
But in truth it would just roll off her back.

Except then he looked into her violet eyes
The sun reflected in tears of grey and blue
Which made him realize this was no mistake
He had come here with a purpose to learn
Even if it challenged or took some time
She knew he found what he desired all along
A being of beauty tainted by a past imperfect
Flawed by friction and heat
That sculpted true magnificence internally
But then concealed it with colorful feathers
To distract from her own vulnerability.

He kissed her softly with small regret
Her tears to him unnecessary and a concern
Yet to her they were part of the healing
Fire, then tears, then love without fear.
She nuzzled him back more open now
Comfortable with him there beside her
Then the rain sprinkled softly down
And for the first time her flames subsided
So, she picked him up and flew effortlessly
To the unadulterated place where time
Would tell their story of unity through grace.

THE RHYTHM OF YOU
March 22, 2005

You play me a song
That I haven't heard before
A melody that lingers
In my flesh and my senses
Long after your pheromones
Erase themselves from
My memory
Too soon.

You tease me with
My own naiveté of
Your enthusiastic world
Where feelings blend
Into mosaics of charges
Electric fantastic erotic
And full like your lips
Their kiss alluring
Haunting and warm.

I trace your features
In my mind to memorize
Them with a soft hum
Unable to decide
What's stronger for me?
Specks of grey that
Penetrate from your eyes

Or the squint that explodes
From them when you laugh.
I'm helpless in my discovery
Fearful that the more I know of you
The more I'll want to sing your song
Over and over and over
Addicted to
The words
The notes
The rhythm of you
That leaves me alone
Wanting
Waiting
Hoping
That maybe
You'll come
Play for me again.

TOUCH OF TRUE DESIRE
March 28, 2005

I want him
Differently but the same
To love and hold close
To need and miss daily
I'm aroused from a space
That exists in my heart
New and unused until now
It's not an intensity of desire
The throw one down and
Rip off clothes before you climax desire
It's a quiet burn that surprises you
When you realize you came already
He makes me laugh from the core
The place where laughter is born
Not the 'just to be nice' giggles
But, the explode with spit
I can barely breathe roars
He loves me softly and secretly
Not too secret, because I see it
In the way his eyes focus on my face
Counting my freckles while he
Figures out what I might say next
As if knowing me better than I know
Myself is his favorite pastime
He won't wait for anything
But, he will wait for sex

To make sure that the magic
We feel together on the inside
Matches the magic spilling over
On our outsides
He touches me with his lips
So, I melt into soft warm sheets
Holding on to him for dear life
Because I know I might not find this again
So, I will enjoy it for every moment
Until the day he walks away
With me still wanting him
Waiting for his return
Unless he chooses to stay instead
Keeping me safe from harm.

SAYS IT ALL
April 1, 2005

We're so polite
So accommodating
We tiptoe through two lips
Afraid to embrace this

I'm ready already
Are you ready?
Tell me you are or
Let's just forget it

Time ticks and tocks
I refuse to watch clocks
As if days passing by
Are laughing at us

You're still there
I'm still here
But, where's the we in us?
It might be time to discuss

You like me
I like you
It's not complicated
It's just difficult sometimes

STEPHANIE LODGE

You get it and I get it
Isn't that nice
But where's the romance?
The gestures of sweetness?

I'm not ready to be
The old married couple
Who stare at silverware
On their anniversary

This is still a celebration
A discovery of excitement
A life of uncertainty found
When one wants to be bound

To someone different then them
Still the same in some ways
That you can't always describe
But, you see plain as day

I'm not afraid
Are you?
Just tell me if you are
So if I must
I can rescue you

From the fear of deserving
The love that we've found

Your voice is my teacher
That orchestrates sound

I'm still here
While you're there
Just waiting to fall
Let's help catch each other
Yep, that says it all.

STEPHANIE LODGE

CAR WASH DAY
April 9, 2005

Gloomy June day in L.A.
The car wash is full again
People have faith it won't rain
A child nibbles on a cracker
The crumbs flying down her legs
Landing on her socks and laces
Another baby waits patiently
Hair the color of carrot soup
Bouncing on his mother's lap
The sound of air jets hitting car windows
Forcing water to run elsewhere
Pierces the hum of the afternoon news
Chairs empty and fill at a regular pace
The cracker baby wants to see what the
Mystery of my laptop is
Entertaining she's sure
Her messy fingers yearn to smudge my
Anti-glare sensitive screen
Traffic full of moving lifestyles
Jets by the clean machines
While I wait for mine to renew itself
Before it carries me to new places
To plant myself and observe
What life has to offer and where
I can find things to experience through
Typed words and an anti-glare screen.

MAD MAN
June 28, 2005

How pissed off he must be
That his watch read half past me
Like he went to bed too early
Then woke up a day too late
With only a shallow memory.

But it wasn't a dream.

It was hard to watch him slip away
Tick tock tick day by day
Don't know why he couldn't stay
When the minutes I became
Fell short of a deeper flame.

And I was looking for fire.

The fuel ran out I guess
Exhausted by the noise of a
Life full of clutter and confusion
Just a mind tortured and at war
With what was out of his control.

But, I wasn't an illusion.

I had feelings left on hold
Stolen thoughts of him left lonely
Warm embraces frozen cold
A lost boy without his Neverland
Flew away from me too quickly.

So, I became the invisible woman.

Then there was the culprit revealed
Jealousy dressed in a jean skirt and heels
Unable to let go of him completely
She reeled him back in discreetly
Until he decided for him she was wrong.

But, by then I was gone.

BLESSED
July 11, 2006

You're witnessing a miracle
That started several months ago
I was sitting in the very last row
Watching poetry I wish
I could TiVo
Because God only knows
What she just said
But I know it was for me
And I have to do that shit.
Even if I'm terrified that
My words just won't penetrate
Like that scared man
Mr. Operate
Who treated me like some tumor
He had to surgically remove
For fear his heart would just plain stop.
Yes, I kill men with my ecstasy
It's what I do
But don't be afraid
I'm gentler with my poetry
You'll leave only slightly maimed
This much I can promise you.

And now the words will come to play
Just like they do every day
So here I am to do away

STEPHANIE LODGE

With the stereotypes of yesterday
Where Love Jones was the only way
The white world knew poetry
As a spoken word escapade
Where voices are displayed
With honesty, integrity and clarity
Inspired by soulful rhythm.
Why yes I am a white girl with a brain
Who knows her tools and what to say

So don't look so surprised.
Oh, and in case you were wondering
No, I'm not some supermodel wannabe
Because I have the height or the face
And I don't want to be some female Eminem
I'm not trying that hard to be cool.
I have my personal sins
Like never playing basketball after school
Did that just to make our coach the bigger fool.
Sure, I could have for the money or the fame
I could have just so that everyday
Someone asks me I'd have the luxury to say
Why yes, I used to be a Spark

No, I'd rather just sparkle on my own
Thank you very much
And I don't have the need to
Come up here and prove something to you

Beyond just being me.
Because isn't that really all there is
In our lives...our current reality
When we make plans
And God just laughs
Because he just doesn't
Give a damn

Come on, you know deep down it's true.
Our existence is enough for him
Reflecting her brilliance
Like the angles in a diamond
Cut with delicacy and precision
And strong from the pressures
Of sex, drugs and clueless parents
Who set expectations
That makes the core indestructible.
But the surface transparent.

That's why these lights sear through my flesh
To my bones that are the same
Color as yours
My core is your core
Even if my brilliance
Might be a different hue
It still shines in beauty and
Both gems have their value.
But, what's really true is that

You are God
So am I
Let's get over it
It's time to remember our divine membership
Of a pattern and a purpose that we
Chose to forget
So that we can all make excuses
Of why we fail to cooperate
Why we fail to truly love each other
Or identify our higher purpose
To look out for one another.
Instead we steal, lie cheat and kill
So that maybe that inner void of dissatisfaction
One day can be filled.
But it won't until we recognize
That we all make up the fabric of her design
With different threads intertwined
Velvets and corduroys
Silks and wools aligned
Woven together in a tapestry
Of continents, countries and states
But we missed our divine purpose
Didn't we?
To keep the planet warm and safe
Because threads they unravel
Fabrics they do get frayed
Just like feelings are hurt
And love gets chipped away.
Oh, and I guess forgiveness

Lost its invitation to the
Worldwide pity party.
Where only the strong and powerful
Step up to the open bar.

In the absence of love
Fear creeps in
Like the snake in Eden
My original sin
Where the image of man
Destroyed the goddess of woman
Because a womb that was sacred
Became a bomb that was human
In the form of a book
That launched a thousand wars
Not the face of one woman
Or the bodies of whores
Instead the mind of an ancient politician
Who thought power was control
Got rid of nature as man's wonder
Got rid of the feminine world
That knew better than to fight with fear
When love was a stronger weapon
Why did he do this?
Because he wanted to create a heaven
Something to aspire to
Something to live for
Reminding us that we are imperfect
Just the way we are

STEPHANIE LODGE

But some of us know better
We look within instead
Finding our inner heaven
We fight the words inside our heads

So you see this is a miracle
A design of the divine
A woman standing in front of you
Never intending to take the time
To show you that beauty isn't skin deep

It runs through to the core
Of what we do and what we say
As reflections of the whole
And now there is one person
Sitting in this room
Looking for their miracle
To stand up on their own
And I invite them to discover
What I knew from before
That speaking the truth
Of your intention
Manifests into so much more
A powerful union that's eternal
From this life to the next
Woven out of freedom to express

And I am blessed.

MY CANDY MAN
November 14, 2007

Brown flecks of sunshine in his
Green lollipop eyes
Irresistibly sweet
He melts my ice cream until it's a
Puddle of goop on the floor
Between my pixie sticks
Tied with red licorice lace
My candy man sticks to your heart
With words like
Hug Me, Be Mine and Luv U
A Romantic man stolen from the dreams of Mr. Wonka
Every girl's fantasy of charm and strength
Like taffy pulling your teeth together
I like my men a bit sour sometimes
And he fits the bill there too
Tart gazes of burning cinnamon bears
Dancing in his eyes
I'm forced to look away until my
Sweet tooth returns
Licking him from head to toe with lips parted
Oh boy can the candy man can
And he does
Every time.

STEPHANIE LODGE

MENTAL MAGIC
September 1, 2009

Like a snowflake I am unique in my design
Microscopic, infinite creativity am I
I am cold, intricate and delicate in this form
Then like magic, in an instant, I transform
With a single shift of a degree
I am a raging flood of uncertainty
Yes, this too is me.

I melt to merge into the quilt once again
Cycle of rebirth through patches of night sky
That shines starlight into my very being
The reminder of home pulls me upward
As I create a new shape from dust and ice
Ooh, this does feel nice.

Then in a blink of a cloud's eye
I tumble back to earth
To join the other flakes
Flurries and storms of disbelief
While the vapor inside me collapses under pressure
My thoughts condense into love and laughter
This time, I am not quite cold enough to freeze

Like a raindrop I am unlimited potential
To become river, lake or sea
I am warm, invisible boundless energy
Then like magic, in an instant, I transform
With a single shift of a degree

I am a joyful pool of clarity
Yes, this too is me.

I turn to mist and vaporize
Into a cloudy haze of newborn mind
Where mentality meets reality in a single breath
Then beliefs become patterns of what I see
The fear washed away by what I am
And what I choose to be
I am God, love, life, air, tree
Yes, this too is me
Then like magic
In this instance
I am free.

ABOUT THE AUTHOR

This is Stephanie Lodge's first published work. She is also an energetic healer and spiritual channel. As an Emissary for Archangel Zadkiel, she works primarily with the violet spectrum of what she terms the *Angelic Light Stream* to 'stream' in new information for the New Era.

She is the producer and co-host of the radio show "Angels in the Buff" and creator of *Halonetix*, a pioneering healing modality that combines the science of Pulsed Magnetic Frequency and the spirit of Angelic Energy Medicine.

Stephanie lives in Sherman Oaks, CA with her husband KJ Lodge and her beloved dog, Shanti.

She is currently working on a series of young adult novels.

Contact Stephanie via email at:
angels@stephanielodge.com

You can also visit her website:

www.stephanielodge.com

www.ingramcontent.com/pod-product-compliance
Lightning Source LLC
Chambersburg PA
CBHW071717090426
42738CB00009B/1805